Throw Out the Life Line
Lay Out the Corse

Personally, I think that this is the biggest load of rubbish I have ever read in my life. It is my 49th birthday today and i have been reading voraciously since I was 5 years, old. I love reading. I have read Zane Gray westerns that were better than this. Its not because its poetry (it actually isn't). It is disjointed burblings that remind me of the writings of people with paranoid Schezophenia as a diagnosis.

However, try it for yourself and see if you enjoy it!

A Critic!

ASA BENVENISTE

Throw Out the Life Line Lay Out the Corse

Poems 1965–1985

Anvil Press Poetry

Asa Benveniste
4.5.84

Published in 1983
by Anvil Press Poetry Ltd
69 King George Street London SE1O 8PX

0 85646 098 2

Printed in Hungary
by Szeged Printing House

This book is published
with financial assistance from
The Arts Council of Great Britain

Contents

As a Valediction *7*

I Starting Lines
pages 11–49

II The Alchemical Cupboard
pages 53–57

III Middle Years
pages 61–105

IV Tabellae Linnaei
pages 109–126

V North Light
pages 129–142

Acknowledgements

As a Valediction

I have omitted from this collection two early books: Poems of the Mouth *and* The Atoz Formula; *also several, though not many, poems which I now find boring. In place of* The Atoz Formula *I have included the long poem* The Alchemical Cupboard *which, as I recall, concluded the study I was engaged in for ten years into the sources of Kabbalistic congruities. It was something of a black period in my life, and when I stepped out of that space I moved on to the ground of light which language anyway has always been for me. But now more so. Most of the poems here have a basis in domestic experience, though it may be hard to believe, and this may explain my treatment of that subject with an irresistible and concerned silliness; domestic life lends itself easily to a complex comedy of language. Language is one of the words which occurs in these poems over and over. Light is another. Syllable, syntax, he, she, you (I am all of them, even in love poems addressed to women who have enthralled me) are others. And the definite article without which I cannot write poetry, though I have tried.*

Almost all the poems here make me smile. I take death seriously, of course, as many people do, but it's not enough to lay it on the line and assume it makes one (you) cower at the majesty of its power, its incomprehensible structure and lastly its divine inevitability.

I have dated these poems 1965–1985. The former is certainly true, the latter something of an exaggeration. But 20 is much tidier as a gematrian *truth than, say, 11, 13, 16 or 17. You must already know that we all lie, and these dates are an instance of what a friend once called 'true lies'. I am implying in that time span poems I have not yet written. Also, superstitiously perhaps, moving into the future in that way may help towards assuring it. I have stopped believing that when I die the world will also end since it gets its existence only from me, an aberration I have enjoyed for at least 30 years.*

I wish I could make my dedication of this book singular and uncomplicated by naming only one, but I have been torn happily by so many friends (some of whom I have also disliked at times) that I can only list them here as they have appeared in my life and allowed themselves to be left there: Abraham Rogatnick, *Lionel Ziprin, Mason Hoffenberg, Themistocles Hoetis, Pip Walker, Jack Hirschman, David and Tina Meltzer, Tom and Val* Raworth, *Peter Jay, John Latimer Smith, Bernard Stone, Ivor Cutler, Phyllis King, Jeff Nuttall, Amanda* Porter, *Dick and Jackie McBride, Agneta Falk especially and all those who have been concerned and skilled with the* material *of printed words on the material of paper, some of whom I have named before in another book. Any others also who have slipped through the net. As Mallarmé may have said somewhere, a poem should not have a beginning, middle or end. It's all words, the lowest form we have and the highest.*

I

Starting Lines

the journey is always anti-clockwise
– Tom Raworth, from 'Reverse Map'

Title Poem From the Author's Posthumous Collection 'Lay out the Corse'

He tenders his gland together
with 0.5 pollen of daffodil – no, 0.8
ah! science! I address you with the fact
that lethal gas rises from the five books
of splendour in the morning
post everywhere announcing
herons have begun to leave
the province of Choan
you come early and I wish to say
you are a part of the conflict
in my mind
the neighbours voices as well as that
get nearer and pause before
the visitors recite Aragon
they chip away at the house
with cake knives
                    beautiful day
to land on the moon
I hear them advance
the sheer skill of sequence
chip chip I'm back again
to reveal desultory things
about Spain
            ¡Aragon! *salaud*

Who Left the Door Open

for John Latimer Smith

Yellow paper conceals akkadian scribe
(o english landscape
once in every poem)

again
(o englische landschaft
un fois chaque poème)

navigation by blind goddess
he ruins his sleep
testing purities of water
cylinder seal 3.8 centimetres
high again at side of page
and assumes a seasonal mask
of bristles and cheekbone

still with too much syntax

Finished for today he takes cap in hand
screws it over writing edge
reads telegram thus:
YOU HAVE BEEN CO-OPTED
TO GENERAL COUNCIL
LINE SPACE

or thus:
CONGRATULATIONS FATHER OF
ELEVEN POUND BABY ASTEROID
LINE SPACE

and notes connection
between this and subjective
weight at birth
o signature of sender

A History of Surrealism

(using schema 3:3:4:4)

Oh well the cyan ink has knocked over everything
just when the ship's compass began to announce
messages of samadhi over the brain waves

so really it reads as follows
Est-ce que je n'ai pas laissé mon parapluie
Hier soir dans votre porte-parapluie?

Uppercase for your oracle method!
though I use a way of looking into museums
stuffed dinosaurs and invitations to join
St Paul's parish community swing

Incidentally just in time
you must not go out of your way
to believe one single word of Max Jacob's
entire death poète d'aujourd'hui

The Wild, The Awful, The True

Suddenly that greed of poetry
a damp smell from the bricks
                                        (brickwork)
as I emerge from sleep
right up to signs of rain
or failing that to signs
of cattle

The race is about to multiply

Schopenhauer at the roadside
counts little cars that use the A145
with mother sunshine in the trees
that died about a hundred years ago
That's Philosophy   That's Life
I'm beginning now to tell you
about the awful dream

Looked up diagram of girl & other sections
the noise of chairs
                                        do you remember?
like ships unload cackling dog?
all those limitations?
I refrained from writing poems
yesterday the light sent the wind
                                        (downtrack)

Break (close) turn away
she rises from the sacrifice
                                        in fragments
length of line determined by paper
dimension of page
                                        heart disease
I work myself into a priest
even the grass
                                        is a dotted line

Key

One familiar two familiar etcetera
I've used them often every day
hardly any colour releases the middle door
at home and once in an emergency
opened the petrol tank though I tried
that before I came and failed
                                        a bad way
to start

SETTING THE SCENE

Sat with you before you left
into the corner of my eye
quiet potman (old english) soft
arab slippers picked one key
(bags of instinct) out of twenty
on the ring opening a cupboard
of irish whisky
                                no hesitation at all
as if that's what really happened

in my dream

PART FIVE

Walked up steps to front door
                                opened outward
                                                        unexpected
lights on all over the house
flashing music from central chimney
dashed down one corridor
                                rooms either side
and out the back
                                sunlight
                                                grass lying flat
                another and
                another
room
walked up   front door
each house opened into sunlight
grass lying flat
                                on the ground

BIOGRAPHY OF THE POET

Everyone thinks in keys
sunlight referred to many times
not once devourer of plants & water
I want to say colour eating colour
cannibal snail iridescent at my door
with a first collection of calcific poems
too late for poet of the seventies
but he might make magician his crown

LATER

Small traces of number & letter
                                        gematria
'shot through with figures
from the chivalric tradition
this fine simile
Midrash to Ruth referring
to the Torah as a nut'
                                        ten minutes
to get through the 45 concealments of God
the house (again) applauds   like a crazed
                                        orchard of birds
                                        planted in broken glass

Specifically Sexual

So finally we approach the last haunches
wavy lines which go out to the *pilotte*
amorous is the most meaningless
of all
        Oh God everybody tells me
to keep it simple   still   my mouth
is beginning to have a life of its own

With several more english to follow
in stupefaction I watch the worm
go down on her hairy epithet
always shifting incorrigible metaphors
just one simple image and then... well
the impression stick falls continuously
at the wrong time

                    she comes to me now
through the field of Chuang Tzu's
second stanza
        the illusionary fishes poem

Three Cartoons

New Years Eve

Today I made an attempt to examine
her pubic hair *preliminary* to breakfast
No success
No blame

As it is New Years Eve
within the boundary of London
AMY LOWELL (small caps) I cry!
                                        ding
              dong

My Secret Life

They were not a bit
like whores in dress
appearance or manners
and my acquaintance
with them opened
my mind to the fact
there is a large amount
of occult fucking
going on

Writing It Down

I return querida
we face each other again
shadows I put of you on paper
never change

                              to put it another way
swallowing flies is not only
love's prerogative

First Words

I don't remember writing the word christendom before
and except for 'tribe' won't trouble you
with O E D definitions
                              other words come to mind: however
is one of them: cocktail: temperature falling:
cunnilingus: power failure –
                                        but 'armoire'
is closer to the truth! ah! the efficacy
of transformation: the ability to transcend
ethnic differences: *la lune* for example belongs to
Houston Texas and the tricks some poets play
on their wives –
                         I love you Maud
I hope we meet sometime quickly
on the way to Wimbledon

Reckoner

This is where the first line should be
In the past I kept everything I wrote
silences pauses comments on the rehearsal
e.g. seventy-six old penny ha'pennies
calculated on innumerable scraps of paper
littered my room gradually littered
my house gradually littered my work
sat down to breakfasts of litter
across my wife's breasts as you know
the streets are getting impossible
Sixty miles outside the city
I walked through a field where goats
were eating mountains of scrap paper
some of which contained calculations
in my own hand:
                    nine shillings & sixpence, right?

A Manual for Pilots

As it goes without saying
wind at the side of house
garbage or be careful to weigh
the serious implications of dreams

Signal for first flood of colour

The blah blah click splash penetration
five p m rain and then it's caution
for undue influence of numerology
lovelife allied subjects

At this point the Duke of Chou
to remind us of less rhetoric
a true effort towards more image
the long roman wall around Essex
ice as they say beginning to form
on the southerly trigrams

What can he do with all that dust?
there are so many American poets
(I mean pilots) just waiting
on the back of tomorrow's tortoise
in jasmine corridors who question
after question

Blue

if you lose anything
        when you get past
            the city limits
make sure it's your language
        giant elms
            milestones
                my heart
has always been part of you
        and now
            across 3000 seas
                of wet rock
the generals are losing
        a battalion a day
            so much
goes into writing a poem

I take what returns
        out of the far-flung
            sephiroth
                and secondly
when we breakfast together
        in easy reach
            of daylight
not knowing if I've picked up
        your spoon
            or mine
                and the point is
I've lost my place

But someday I'll read a whole book to you at one sitting:
        kings coming out of the eastern oceans
            with blue-mouthed magicians
                and all the plants we never see
as though pine took root on my palate
        spreading over the whole house
            leaves us covered all day
                flowing with yeast
over the turned-rim syntax of our bed

Arousing

Abysmal

There is a way of waiting

Dangerous spheres with nothing in them
but pale couch grass
        young rodent   apparently so near
crossing the traffic of cities
blind with rain   blackout
        a sense of fish getting through my fingers
the way your hair changes colour as you speak
touches such things as
                        divination

I am certain I wrote one poem that year
leaning the Ching up against all the other evidence
                                        waiting for sunlight
to illustrate the dimensions of my fright

So much for waiting

Instinctively I know which questions to ask
Tonight you advanced through the door backwards
        and showed me the stool's ouroboros
impressed on your arse
        reminding me of our marriage
        I was reading the passage
concerning superior men who deliver themselves
of their great toe
(fortieth hexagram
                thunder
                        over
                            water)
If you have *never* believed me
the ramifications are endless

For example see how long the pyramids take
holding death down to a cypher

and not even (cup your eyes)
as if it were rotting flesh
vaulted deep in those fermenting deserts
laid out to ease   waiting
in a way that sweet company over
the ocean's rock came into our house
together
through the wardrobe of our sleep

Change

Curve of your thigh in touch with light
at this point
                    language
                                  an arithmetic
of plates on the kitchen floor thrown
in a random rage as though you hadn't heard
or unanswered
asleep
        sleeping

When I came in again the light was flickering
I've finished anyway reading my poems to you
what more do I want
      seeing your body in print
            watching the film that goes on
between your legs
                              life isn't always a matter
of choosing the right moment
often the armies ride over ransacked bridges
                                        and we in between
that plundering at the head of each militant hexagram
aethyrs out of the Great Key of Solomon

This is dream language

How can you hope to make any revisions
coming back into the room
            without any light
        now
but white body at the profile of our bed
sharp fall of breasts against this document
with fish laid at the sabbatical of fingers
up to my sucking lips
                                    and I am taken in
like an amateur
a cretin on the ground
of that long loping love

Sprung Song

Then follows Canaan and other acts
of mercy beautifully described endlessly
detailed
        What *is* it I'm after?
always the both of us always two

He makes straight for
'They touch one another in dreams'

She addresses her remarks to Canaletto
and steps out into the winter rain

Then follows Ashtoreth the open cut
spilling forth its purple wardrobe
just to be home
                they like the old poems best

        Listen it's me before I forget
in sleep to each other
across the long forage

Blockmaker's Black

He views the black girl
through his fingers
totally in dream
she resists half tones

this is nervous printing

outside the colours are
well, different, somehow,
looked up, waited
for questions from
the even distribution
of green and blue
illustrations

New Writing

With the best intention I am about to start
a description of lions who sun themselves
in the black gorse at nightfall gather gather
draws his arm across sweat there's hardly time
before the next poem the river the girl in that order
who cannot wait to give herself completely to ice
the distance between patisseries that's *real* travel
awake during the inverted commas of open space
the sea washes up hanging so much dust along the hammering
eye the haunches the burning thicket the ancient mound
of her belly the two constellations the milky way
of her throat the tongue of song in her mouth
                                        I tell you
I never want to escape the book of words
no matter how much love is showered on my mane

Mise en Scenes

1.
The season starts with Garibaldi

Whoever heard of driving horsepower
through the groundplan of Italy
when body action (any word will do)

2.
The cinema devours the lion the lioness
the tiny Bokhara rugs
                                        it is my duty
to alarm the coprophagists

3.
Obscurity I love it
in Genoa watch how many
words come rumbling out
for the first time containing
the following English such as

4.
FELICITY
standing
in its own
ground

5.
So many foreign languages to learn
lines traced around the murder victim
turns out a plan of back home
Stop the burning cauldron!
Giuseppe's soprano has just said
I lug you

6.
Why does he do it?
He does it because
he is desperate
My Lord
desperate

The Greek Anthology

to Peter Jay

Don't bother me with Heraclitus
who reveals a fragmentary greatness
of thought
                    moving on to Li Po
who tipped his arse at the moon
and fell into a bucket shop in Baltimore

                    I cannot justify anything
concerning Demeter goddess of corn
as long as connections are being made
and since we're out in the country
falling under the Virgilian sky
in the distance those lights
are a tail end of the province
of Delaware
                    being crossed
by the crazy dactyl Washington

but I don't really see it myself

Cours de Civilisation Française

I cannot help it
if one line follows
on logically
from the next
regard the purity
of tone the placement
of each phrase inevitably
upon the forthcoming:
mouse mickey french
and the secret life
of Paul Fort
not forgetting
apes throughout Paris
who recently enthused
over crime passionnel
and from the first mouthful
they spoke
                poulet surprise

Certainly Metaphysics

In certain descriptions I notice certain words occur
over and over unassailed non-argumentative benign
I am not afraid to play the part of Chinese emperor
and do not believe it is the easiest way to wisdom
there are some shapes we fill without entering into
for example language is one of the body limitations
for example my engagements outnumber my pleasures

That said I have begun to realise already
this is one of the key poems one of the description poems
outside this room in which we get extremely good reception
it will almost certainly snow although I hesitate
what appear to be certain floating fragments
in the air similar to the outline anatomies
similar to certain religious encroachments

Poem

1. *The Text*

He does not want this to have any connection
with *chinese* poem all about calligraphy
rain on his cube of ink he writes
'cloud slants across the Greater Rockies
reflection of good life on earth
                                                        scars on the face'
somewhere along the sequence of earlier heaven
a poem has to have

2. *The Commentary*

'rain on his cube of ink'
he speaks of his diminishing powers
and how often his (and others) death
one way the light changes tracing
the carnal comforts from east to south
to north
          reflection: nice word
for loyal servant
NEVERTHELESS
a poem has to have a certain solemnity

At the Court of the Yellow Emperor

with the sky dropping slow in the sky
frame of trees
                a small leaf in my whisky
watch how he brings in landscape references
Have you noticed it's autumn outside, they said?

seasons all over again my breath weathers
at the window looking out for brown rust
that gathers on my hands
so much time away from home I remembered
twisting the cap off the jar you failed at
didn't forget to say thank you
before finding a way
                        out of my wide-flung sleeves

Umbrella

in memory of Weldon Kees

then during the apollonian trial
he succeeds in describing exactly
the shape of the umbrella
he opens his throat from cylinder to arc
losing all motion halfway between
the curious gallop
a bowl a dome the yapping dog
it's to be found in the words he choses

but not just the shape

his discourse includes Salonika
pink melons old inscriptions
China's emperors who consign
rank and service to ministers
by the circumference of their shade
whatever they learn duplicates
in their throats
                    love also
pursues the same deception

he claims it is now too late
for any of the voices to be accurate
green friezes stacked loosely against
the wall a clatter of stalks
error being a description
what he stoops to is both display
                              and divination

the light is changing
our poems are about poems
he enters through the window
opening an umbrella
stops reads starts again
changes the first line

and goes back to it
                    over and over
the wind has already begun
to rattle the new pages

Georgic

They ascend from still wheat
off the horizon
biblical radius the sky darkens
I don't feel much these days anyway
flies popping from my eyebrows
which is about all that can be said
for history

and one other fact:
the transplantation of yarrow
from China to English verges
on deliberate botanical

poem

A Passing Description

The mist comes down suddenly
throwing a ring across the field
in front of his eyes so much is true
he looks for fire the just element
dog barking & other than that
silence the chinese sage perceived
along museum walls through glass
pine silk the country continuum
I have invented this room
just as I have imagined the placing
of Norfolk pools of dense water
that rest on the surface of every page
it is winter my flesh is too thin
for this flat monosyllable of ground
he has already kissed away all apparent
green outside where a sequence
of running heads with sufficient knowledge
to perform each nameable transmutation
O God I love your words

Tu Fu

vessels of joy
tea smoke
putrefying grain
into liquid
& to the other
declivity his age
tracing outward
elements
the first nudging
at his T'ang empire
712 to 770 during which
1,457 poems 32 grass
pieces and seams listing
a crazy old man
but decorous
with wine
and always 2 graphs
for the same definition
the others being compassion
a strict servitude
frugal service
to the state
and a hatred
of rebellion
'so what we are we do not'
aperture
channel of image
servant   carrier
always starting
long poems
finishing
short

Resembling Words
Resembling Sculpture

for William Turnbull

old saw horse chinese mogul
turns to his wife
                    two by four planks
laid square across horizontals
and sees for the first time
not old but newly pinned with pivotal silence
grooved and plugged grain
facing directional vertices
which establishes the letter M
we arrive at another crossroad

he explains that Mahler performs
an acceptance of the word *I*
so in describing the form above
his hand does not go near a tool
Canada pine the sea flooding
slowly inundates words concerning
transmutation which begins with
gauze-breasted women of T'ai-yuan
their speech organs

It's the Same Old Feeling Again

1 The Jealousies

We start by knowing what glues together
and what locks without the aid of circuits
it's important to fly throughout the body
of information iron railings on my left
other runners already spots against
my right arm kissing each word
as it emerges from the image park
this is something to do with collision
in the face of extreme pleasure
and a way to get round the new seasons

2 The Decencies

Lie together is already an ambiguity
easier to face easier to avoid
she understood *everything* he said
they looked to the front door to break
a noisy exchange of references
plastic models airplanes vintage poems
old windy waiting stage the point is
sunlight streams through to the design
and effects the music traversing its way
into the life of my audial bushes
yes

Railway Poem

enter & ride this particular poem for example
inevitably turning left round the railway junction
the most beautiful girls are those
who gyrate in free boredom
episodically with welcome arms
and open sandwich courses
                                        Mother
as you can see I have discarded
those origins except as a simple echo
of my father's voice my father's voice
spring is beginning to appear
in my armpits as an adequate terminus
within the contest of seasons
late morning the absent gesture towards
                                        Prince Chou
at this moment running the coins
somewhere under the eyes of his almond wife

Meet Mish Mush

or Hokusai those blue sunshine strokes
they say who speaks to waiting doors
starting the dream off with rhythm
blue rain blue smoke blue eyes
I've seen her fill the grand canal with birds
before the great release a slag
of poems obscuring the view from inside
'I honour Mish Mush in any medium'
he says mourning his resinous lunch
'she's mind mind all mind'

for Tom Raworth

The History of Trench Warfare

transcending soft enough a care for contours
and travel is *not* one of the considerations
there are dangers
                    in using old paper
for certain types of poem
somewhere else we are having lunch together
in a focussing distance
                        the Aegean is obvious
by the way we speak

mist lies on the road northward
two feet above the warring plovers
I have caught my ear in her mirror music
the battery runs down the wet banks
of her body
              being a plain woman
she carries flowers back to earth
and waits for her own language
one of the rules is to keep the head
below water
              many deaths

Living Unit

You find me counting the number of times
our bodies have crossed in this room
scene change
                    the ringmaster shies
low flying geese the african plain
blossoms into fire
                         and air and beginneth
the word *the*
                  transcending

Domestic Poem

I arrange the texts in front of me
it is almost morning my fingernails trimmed
my hair arranged the way I like it
I take the pistol up to my mouth
and pull the trigger
music starts up again in the mirror
I walk to the window to see the light rising
cars begin to move through the streets
I switch on the coffee beans the lemons the cement
busy busy getting ready for the next visit
o transitive verb o yellow dressed
green eyes brown nipples I blow air
through your thighs and bare bones

The Hedge Man

yes cut cut those
who can mitigate roses
and drill machines
syllables ready to argue
against the tangle of locomotives
we die leaning against generation

suddenly we're left only with woods
and dun dogs that stand hackled
many tracks foliate from this point
we decide there are already
too many beds in our house

coherence is a way of looking
at distant light over brown earth
another manifestation
the next show of nature
starts tomorrow
after the diphthong

Happy Ending

Febrile feeble the stones covered
in gore. I am interrupted
by the word, the thought.
Thread narrow, the play starts
with two knocks and a squealing door.
Isn't that what everyone does,
Mr Joy?

Green

what the serpent said within the garden
I have already outwritten you all
boasting of his lightning satan'az
his mouth in contact with dust
as he moved over the ground
crooked in form who spoke
first after God followed by the woman
and last of all the man
                                        which is what
Nahhash intended
                                    I have already
written all the words in my own dirt
avoiding the grace of smooth surfaces
though he believed himself a beauty
under tappuah
                        the maker
of language
                leveller
who took spheres from his mouth
unto theirs
                so poetical
in seduction click clack
the animals too at that expulsion
finding their own fears

finding their first dreams

II

The Alchemical Cupboard

The Kabbalah, as much as poetry, is the study of and submission to the mysteries of the word. The language used by Kabbalists is so intricately dimensional that it is almost impossible to fully convey the simultaneous layers of meaning revealed in the simplest of words.

– David Meltzer, from 'The Secret Garden'

Its traces (the Kabbalah's) can be found in the period when, back from their captivity in Babylon, the Jews awoke to a new awareness of themselves...

– Carlo Suares, from 'The Cipher of Genesis'

The Alchemical Cupboard

As much for the seatide ages of my sons
                                        your body
  with so many things
    now alone
following
    that ascendant line at which
          I am last of all
                  just to be taken
                  as a jew
                long
            past
        the three stages
fledgling   runner   finally
                          out of the sky
                down from the head
          never to try the sun
again so far mistaking
              distance for clarity

•

Contains a command of all
                  my sexual
                      appointments
                          Bain-marie Mary
                  whose hands
        whose moist thigh
thrown over carelessly
                  my languaged mouth
                      dumb with sucking
                  her body
        hopefully
a sulphurous digression
                  of fire & soaring
                  briefly
                  to the top of my throat
        a sign of calx
    the re-entry into metal

that return to fulgid
earth
(over)
earth

•

& Fludd awakens Paracelsus the skin Pythagoras to Kelly your Dee names Lully who turns Bruno Dellaporta the axis Ashmole of Jabir earth who Hermes smeared Philadelphus across Zosimus my Maimonides tongue Dorn lies Avicenna to Gerard break Abulafia argument of Aquinas city wound Dastin in the Bonus head Wu child against Vaughan the storming Eleazar black Benveniste birth

•

on no account of green names
but of blue in many ways
crucibled
a dark mercury
as though blood
had been added in pollution
herein the only city
putting ink to paper
how they could believe
(altogether)
in transformation
in sullen gold
more than red slime
as near to
martyrdom

•

It is in my poems
which process
planetary notations
a house to be born in
a movement in the eaves
some cupboards
that conceal
recognition

cover names for a prayer
of conjunctions & near misses
a certain shyness
a shading of the eyes
as sun devours lion
symbolic furnace
hermetic bed
50 yarrow stalks
thrown out of the green cup
O blind mother
two-bodied fierce
oration
tsallis at my cheek
the poem stopped as it does
mid meaning

•

            you have your fingers
to Ark so long
that swan bent wrist
shadows my wall
            1925
birth then pummel me back
to time silence is what I mean
when I call it
          flight
the corners of my work
clean clean pymander
shroud from the davening
            machine
raise wings and down
river womb silvergrey fish
we know by familiar
corners in the eye
            talisman
four qualities contains
out of ignorance
            we depart
before we once more fire
gold for kissing

lunar sol
black swan its crucible
snow descends

horizon

•

but the sea
this soft anglo-saxon speak
my head iambic breaks
through devouring water
wasting the coastline
this land
for so many
years
all poems have been
dedicated to
music   contained
rot lute   transparent fingers
there is a colour of honey
which comes out of
body english
& soft winter
changes
time
high
in their
low
scuttled
land

•

So Sepher says
would none the less subsist
would be no time or place
what is here advanced
exist in ideas only
who almost was
more eminent than
but also to the nature
of dependency

The parts of space are
that cannot increase
or diminish but that
in change takes place
which can be imagined enters
and a kind of perception
since without true unities
is dominance my body
the sorcerers bowl stones
in the swaying cot
let fall

Not only to diminish
justice which marked
the figure to hear
this noise as we do
by the motion of this law
like music takes time
ending an open casement
from wardrobe to roof
to field outside
and finally to voices
in the gates
of home

III

Middle Years

Experience is one of the forms of paralysis.

– Erik Satie

Bird Appeal

We are one with nature O!
don't go away rizla never
leave me
            for a start the golden
gouge comes wrapped in ampoules
of mild pain killer for mild
pain
      not as precise as some
social poems perhaps
         or miscellaneous objects

In another description
the sea rages against specific
bananas
           a form of lockjaw
keeps the peanut boats from ever
coming into harbour
                          'craw craw'
the gentle gulls remark
'when will it end?
say when'
            NEVER
says the intuitive arrow
NEVER

The Finger Points to Humid

cloud certainty with occasional square
the repetitious dream the repetitious shape
I begin that awesome heroism
divination

the flood of earthy nomenclature
revising all the river ocean lake references
whenever birds come in under the door
dying with legends totally on the page
such as Shenandoah
weather condition (such as) sharks infest
turning point
the water turns

that side of holy Wensum where is a use
of papier maché rock with palm trees
crinkling away to humid and followers same
it's the age
we live in says the river like nothing else
swelling to overtake combustion engines
engaged over surfaces of carpark
the endurance
of aqueous a stormy tranquility of skies
opening up the knife edge of change

Working with Coypu

mouthful trouble one way to start
finding the only word is adrenalin
in prestigious porcelain the colours
are arranged the following way
yellow cyan magenta black
and white as a repetitious printing
when suddenly the sun shines
one millimetre ahead of the speeding
eye twinkle dead honey many targets

this explains the pica rule
conquistador returning home
with shoes of thin beaten gold
from dust farmer to god
the dark deepens the windowless temple
outside buffalo stampedes have reduced
the exploding coypu to one survivor
referable word hiding in the gutter
and another baby added to the rain figures

Boil

American midwest my plentiful pain
God he cries out if you let me off
with this last one in the armpit
growing like slag I promise to follow
with definitely improved camera work
so much oil underfoot the land
is boiling over with damp richness
buffalo shoes anorak chairs and girls
who haven't heard of sex altogether
but plan ahead anyway as though
the quality of autumn rust-coloured
fixing fences as close as they can get to Ohio

At night I take the other lines up with me
and place them strategically correct
in pairs of local confusion as birds
who find their dead places on the road
late spring young out of warm ruffles
flying along my eyes blink much these days
collision turning point subject matter
edges are as sharp as you find them

Lecture Notes

Visit us soon Gaius Septimus
before the house fills with cries
from Herculaneum already stricken
with pain along the walls bounding
the peach orchards
                                        middle river
The Lecture Notes of Pliny the Elder
Yes in innocence
                                    whose lips
a tautology across stone teeth
flute counter to dry pleasure

Colour comes into this too:
one small achievement each morning
keeping at bay
                                the black translucence

Gravebird

it fails even at collision point
birdbody hank & thick shoal
somehow wheeling along at this speed
tiny black mainsails rising on the soft verges
                                        yes   failure
they have died before in Pliny as I remember
going down fast grit up against
giant screen
          the poem machines
in fine hone contact with
                                        transsiberian concrete
gravelling home at last buried in snow
'candlelight dinner for two' she whispered
328 quails consumed in one
pinny
     noting the tense plurality
whereas some others never reach up the social
for inflatable park poufs at all
looking to planetary light scrape shuffle
'tell me what else is there, Gustave?'
whose life has a certain distinguished
transparency
          in the cadaverous pottery room
kickwheel platform slip glaze and all
such terminology suitable
for crushed flies between pages
of poems
          as she passes in silk
among the windy french poplars
& omen

Cortège

even before the dynasty
has established itself
as quantum
quantum deus
                    shadow
of reeds falls
at the bright lake
contradiction of language

at that moment
when motion
becomes speed

if the grass stirs
there is nothing hidden
within
         the cortège (passing)
like a desirable failure
desirable failure
                    (desirable)

before this I noticed
every hesitation
dash dash
              entre deux mers
the words carry us
the gunwales

Orations

I

After all the decoys
This one is the forest.
Wheee! much goes into
Expression of thrill.

II

Twice I have attempted the word
CONFLUENCE.
This is the final try,
Amadeus.

III

Sun pinging
The adverse chamber,
Delightful pain.
Even in death
It's language first.

IV

Slide hopefully
Towards definition.
Providing the text:
Item from notebook,
1906: moveable type
Already more than
500 years old.

V

The Reversing Poem.

VI

Alignments:
Matrix; mother.
And I mention sacrifice
Only in passing.

VII

The trouble with watching
Too much TV,
You hit all the repeats
Indoors and out.

Middletown, Virginia

The geometry of roses?
I remember Bezalel Loew
accumulated so much rubbish
in the cellar and up they came
leaving their mark on this inn
of distinction enough to last
all those generations ago
there have been many transmutations
since the breakthrough in bombay duck
dimpled paper yes footprints on
the clock tower yes a nasty time
and today there is so much length
of white dog loping loose in the ice
cream parlour when silver propelling
pencils have just about disappeared
out of our lives the older I get
the more etcetera
                              there's no end at all
to the number

To Nudge Avail

off the mirror o dense word hollows
there is much land stubble to get past
before arable which will make sense
of all journeys all seed dwelling
                    what's missing here
is clearly-induced narration
the marauding hill tribes
                              rape loot
new taxes and such like
following the suppression of old forms
of dervish
            in favour of language traffic
the lushness of black the appointment
to assist in minor prophecies
how the earth doth profane itself
with architecture
                    and many forms
of close communion

men do not participate in final payment
'I am not concerned with life after death'
life alters life and in this manner
the earth has eaten upon itself
looking outward to the spin
of nudge availability
                         o tilt
such as now wherever soft
and takes us with ease & readiness
I dedicate to tumbles
                         landfall wind
the deathly sugars incomprehensible humour
snapped branches and all that is done
in divine error

The Collections

snake rock eye bright heliotrope
where *do* all these words?
                                        who thought
he could build a whole landscape
on this
            more like stone on water
less than he has to describe
                                    and only
a track of weather in his
rural scene:
                    cow with marauding cud
paper clip substituting as kerchief
                                        odd man
who walks on flame to well water
lilies flowering in the land brigade
date at the bottom
                                (with self-portrait)
1881: edition two hundred & fifty black
even then some people had a distinct
nostalgia for grease guns
                                        & gibbets

Hunting Desperately Through the Streets of Newcastle

tight as leather
horse bridle
english madrigal
o potboiler
my stack
my spurs
my compline
the train
through fields
of notation
leaves & mulch
thereof
          and mist
settling down
to the charred
banks
        correctly
stoned

Do You Recall the Days of High Tea?

They arrive numerally
figuring ball thumb implements
in flashback the house murmurs
medieval english with currant caps
while in the foreground snow
reclines among formica living pads
one dactyl ending after another
so much quiet surrounding another day
in the roar of lions who oversee
the interruptions

Here we have to be careful about smudge
our susceptibility to language regularities
and all kinds of fire earth water elements
the filling in of detail
which is often referred to as
beautiful braking

Personally I cannot hear this music
without thinking of Caroline going into her act
who realised late in life that she was possessed
by the spirit of Poseidon the greek god
of conch shell and pink inner garden furniture

Early evening he is busy recording
the late sequence of bird baths
four books to his credit and none of it
telling one tiny pivot
of American history
Too bad
this is where the garden ends she tells him
Take it they have already picked the next train
to the land of tabasco
finally

Armless Wonder or Maiming The Names

therein the shape already described
as of detriment lacking a cradle
of arm for the head to drop into
or at times Pavese suffering
the italian summer & those hairless boys
along Via Virgil drawn skin murder
concealed between the optimism of buttocks
griggins watching over a jesuitical
account of intake balanced by expenditure
what has been hoisted in routes out of
Africa the slave goods the broken boxes
poems arriving through the hot mediterranean
and Crashaw who kisses the buttons of Carpaccio
the mastoid effects in Luis de Góngora
Milton ticking his first wife's prognosis
Horace's swollen disc endlessly swathed
Great God! it says in the sky all those telegrams
totally transmitted throughout the golden graft
is there no middle to all this flywheel fire?

Sonatina

The leg drops down
munch!
what am I looking for?
quick search through spines
enthusiasm is one thing you can say
about court music
in this area the east wind
when it isn't threatened by stubble fire
zips in on time
you notice monosyllables

pars secunda
inaccuracies of language
I put this down to an event
in my image susceptibilities
and now to conclude
we have uncovered
this time
so munch

and

no

more

.

Stations

1.

I look for objects to trip over
once round the confinement
                                                        I enter
it is safe
            the cat likes me
likes my cigarette smoke
reflects on the possibility
of different food
this is english poem
said the poem
                        speaking up
for itself in the teeth
of vastly truthful opposition

2.

He looks: the rest of it
is largely lost; I mean
peanuts everywhere brooding
in native honey cakes
the octopus who advances
from one corner
                        into another
corner progressively quickening
his blood temperature
Sleeper! who has risen and
done much damage to my sadness
I celebrate his flashing
duplicity

3.

Camel and herdsman silhouetted
against the sun in Gabes
their prescient traffic with
skilled lips with
                        wind ripple
across the dunes with
                        biblical
                                    paper
                                            cup

o figure flasher
you been here before
breaking balloons
with fire

4.
The cat telephones for sandwiches
here I am faced with socratic
theatre
          we exchange views
on penmanship archery rules so on
'It begins now to appear that no deep
gulf is fixed between life and non-life'

5.
You; You; such an old trick
smoothly the same sequel to language
for the past two nights
I have again dreamed
of the infant queen
                              who watched
her toppling of crass metals
with ease and physicality
throne
          orb
               garment
                              who can refuse
the smallest notation
her tiny fingers
her buttocks smelling of wheat

comes to me as a breaking
of light
          I breathe into her mouth
hold hands kissing while blood
flows from her onto the bed
onto the floor the bright blot
spreading over her whole body
as she rises
               towards

Paper is just Paper and not the Tablets of Moses

simple
the line already catches
heavy breasts not like silence
simplicitas
written on alien bandage
caravan trail of lust
rain a thousand privileges
upon the stallion
sultan spares life all around himself
and returns to Monkey Mount

changes of pace
part one long meditation
second short percussive
third part diction:
'He had small regular teeth
each one like the other'
is there so little
to that angel's mouth?

OM

this is not the first time
I have welded my lines
cutting outward from darkness
into the machinery of your wrist
and with such speed who grazes
from this shelf on pastures
of breath and live cutters
that I have subsequently
returned from posthumous poems

                              in the distance
where you have defined heaped ashtrays
with dotted cries of the flag
russian warships bear down upon
disparate wife and her vestal
charges in smoke and byzantium
o camel-faced companion of the stove
blind stitcher they imagine also
that I tamp meaningless sequences

under syntactical weight grass bends
so much body piling up
pineal reports and readings of Racine
on Jade Mountain that french
son et lumière spit curler
Say hello Osip
                    Arthur Waley you too

Mute Leader

surmounted by butterflies sleeping asses
and thick rainwear assigning tickets
to aragonese boxes where visitors
familiar in deep religious fat tango
to the music of gematria
        this is where it all fails
I have prevented my orchid visitation
waiting on the edge of leaf signs
small prophecy fulfilments
in an area pointing to structure
otherwise travel holds no psychic
achievement passing on a treadmill
blue outlining heaven the painted
eucalyptus and sailing craft that go
out into sprockets of total cliché

Original Turkey Mill

what he must be doing
harrowing the first green spikes
grass script uncoils
yet everything he does
is history my dear Mother
now we are at the forest
that left hand of mine active
in image as always smudge
from America the fool writes
'I never understood your work
but so poetical'
as in the smear of Izmir
oh well
O Well!
It visits upon me
my chances to explain
growing less
                    truthful
for example

as in the tease of white tuberoses?
flute? taw? turkey
trot?

Microtonal

Subject to perspiration
he shifts dust from one place
to another

Everybody is talking at once

The ruff more complex in its attitudes
'the book belongs to the book'

He farts a lot being so much alone
broadly speaking – *la liberté de péter*

Room full of sound
flies at the re-enactment of honey
he listens to parallels

Spends most of the day
determining style for his face

his poems

Side B: time notation
The Helvetian Episode

Lost Poem

word and whorl these the spiral
one of green one trans
parential
            as to style:
water
        dark growing from light
an old poet draws heavy lines
through all image confluence
the excised dances
black smell of burning
the music the the the
                                these

codicil: no dash between date
of birth and date of death
but a hyphen short close breadth
diagonal ends
                    geometrically
a parallelogram
as in Garamond
'the bruised face'

Colour Theory

this gesture of knives
left behind rusting
in otherwise bare
country rooms
                    byzantium
the beginning of icons
relates me at once
to the sanction of your eyes
brown metal on brown floor
the homing of milk goats
tamper of small parallels
the contiguous spill
of tongues

here now I come upon it
as a maker of street songs
my own white on white collar
rolled to infinity
within the facial arc

Colour Theory: The Application

she saw her father's complexion
as an extreme of madder
                                        deletion
a waste of her burning room
too many facets of orange
                                        outside
blue pane of ice moving downward
covers through glass the poem frame
under hard rexine blocking
                                        this is home
it takes her to its cold entrance
dips at the form of her father's tongue
she madly vacant in the piazza
uterine canal her bright mind deaf
to the limp labia of Dublin
                                        soft line endings
Gallic definitions rubbing at the last trace
of skin
        of image

Coloured Mansion 1474

poet machining new concepts at Bruges
and in his literature a deformed knowledge
of extracts pried at the shapeliness
of heavy impression 'ink in a deep valley'
deployed over the transparent unicorn
which meeting of metal and vellum he remembered
had once occured to him before and would again
that rubble of speech in his songs
never a full line but a kind of utterance
a stab of prayer already templated
within his own dream and within mine

now that it is over between them: Man: God:
or whatever matrix cuts the eye
O fibrous Egypt you will conclude
this codicil by walking over posthumous ice
pursued by naiads hoping to drag you
into the serifs of blind paper

Honfleur

Light begins to hamper the room
the book closes
                    and when
releasing the captive violin
so like morning black
cold words exact spaces
this is it she interrupts
                that's just it
think of that
                and others in the room
understand the first obstacle
has been breached

mathematics serious language
float across years of honoured
abstract
          (no no wrong wrong
start here
          she leans towards me
her hand over her mouth
I cannot hear what she tells me
so simple
            I love you?
WRONG
            all the wrong books
            the birds so fierce
            under black tiles
I have kept out of this
as long as I can
                    Where were *you*
Satie?

Summer Poems for Mallarmé

so still
fruit fly
passes my face
the air stirs
the telephone
hot against
my silent mouth

I go out into the street
to this day
              my friends still
find knowledge in the miracle
of Lazarus

---

the serrated moth appears
again afternoon light
an entry in my journal

'infinite gentleness'
colour captures repetition
language becomes simpler

you who attribute its appearance
to the power of broderie anglaise
closed books everywhere in the room

he writes the way he speaks
'desireless' *soul lennei*
even now in thick bud

a small plane passes over
becomes
          sound

Note Tone

bull frog
I should have written
down what you said
my symbiotic thumb
also full of pain
confused you with *frig*
why is it they cheer
whenever you ace
into the obtuse corner
of that king's court
but when I do the same
the error is mine
blamed for your sacred
incompetence
because
I love myself
approximately
six minutes
per annum

Translations

so much of that breech poetry
mute inquisition
old lines
bone pressed against bone
flame devouring flesh
the gradual turn of the river
old Tu Fu dies of fever
travelling alone by boat
(winter 770) having already
renounced his muddy
cup of wine
my window overlooks
a blind corner in the road
where cars not knowing what
they are up against
sound mad warnings
old lives
I am back to playing
in the street pitching pennies
up against the school wall
bald
watery
skinny words

Moist Ash

1. How to use words

there are those which begin:
poem as an approach to curvature
one way is to scramble taoist
a dog say makes itself agreeable
to God
          others honour the word *distinction*
a success somewhere in prosodic
statement as it overtakes *serious*
                                        (or *transcendence*)
for example: that's that

2. Vernacular

so much
for that
summer light

end of day
time
being

I think
while light
thinks

he enters
they
house

when we
meet we
change

what is past
is total
divination

the real poem
is already
in the bag

The Subjunctive Poem

gravity feed
circuit twice
to discover
a firm
connection
at the most base
                    dead Crashaw
                    thrown young
                    the pines

in another way
to break this
Carthaginian
silence

reading back I find the words
cut cut
                referring to flowers

wild menthol
Odessa
                when I have learned
this craft well enough
to take up Nike's
sledge

the news from London
is gravel pit
and eagles hammered
on the swages
not as fact but as
contingent

that being one way
to deal with it

Anoxia

Hell, what chance do I have
5 minutes 30 seconds without breath
and then when the screams began
grew into my crabbed left hand
and this particular damage
of scribbled lines every day
all over the house
my mother telling me
from her blind eyes
watch out!

Dense Lens

A reasonable sequence of 10 poems...

– Doubleganger

1
Pound's Planchette

no mindprint will ever equal
japanese dancing establishments
activiste sleep dealer the great
unfolding of paper forest as dust
slopes across gaunt innocence
another way of saying this is to say
that we admire wisdom too soon
the frequency of splintered edges
falling at one's touch
the repetitions

                    and many years spent
between the wars in Hollywood
teaching the first gestures
to restaurateurs child actors
its word should not have been motion
the sequence changing into a seated
man who converses with a four-inch
spider scurrying into sunlight stopping
scurrying stopping
                        the book opens
folio 232: the apparitions of Michio Itow

2

Buck's Box

This is the bad end of town
Bad!
        what's called a late flowering
cracked adobe under the fingerprints
tin silos salt reaches
lots of sucking and stucco
wondering how the first dream
come up on the first frames
Buck Jones who writes two or three
poems at the same time
1 upstairs
2 under the yucca tree
3 high in the saddle
a plea for the goodness of Arkansas
on his lips enduring pain
at the old friction of Melanie
or Black Honey or the smash of war
o spring what courage you have
to ease open the cold sphincter
the poem being dead

3
Meat Page

in my musical adventures with a pause
for praising parades in Oslo pack sleds
and snapping brave coolies
we are off now to say hello
to this special chapter in which the dolby
system is such a great influence
on sound slam and hiss using
all the loop possibilities
the structure does demand

this involves country living as a first sign
of enormous beauty bearing down
I will never hear again so much eat
action in so many indicative languages
o my life
what impressionable time has been spent
framing every image with smiling
white teeth

4

What is Art? The Hero in Man Says Josephus

and then he remembers a long line stretch
something between flowers the bull ring
and a song from the Cheyenne nation
trying to come up to all those old gods
sandblasted from the stone of honour
ceased to be added to and meanwhile
brows arched in the half light
neighbours beating the bare earth
with their dusty feet
Part One
Hector buckles his bronze thorax
and sets himself round
the shaft of his spear
He will soon be dead
Part Two
Thunder Horse placing his men
high along the surrounding hills
He will soon be dead
Part Three
The cigarette sparks off an equinox
in the poet's right hand
while his left writes
He will soon be dead

5

Punctuation Enters from the Left

Thus (the motion then being frozen
it arrived through the door
just as the apple bite *took place*
Alliluyeva or something equally true
since she is so beautiful
in the twilight assembly
                                        alternatively
she commits me to a quiet natural
lunacy such as the fault which runs
into the volcanic glaze the deep crag
and iron horse (parallel to this
the circle of grizzly hirsute toothful
portuguese including myself crushing
with their feet the summer harvest
in giant mildewed vats (or do I mean
toothless
                that is how a poem is formed
said the bitten apple
                                    (or do I mean
The Bite: which precedes all

6
Smiles: Shooting Script

Alluding to lump molde
in the hungarian graph book
135×95 mm prior to a great
sliding elusive trim
just let it leave
its illimitable way
by the tokaji peninsula
scratch scratch scratch
the music a crescendo
with giant shoe traces
along the galaxy
and blind spots marking
minutes and many kilometres
up to the sunny clapper
which reads: Low Crow:
Take Sixty-nine:
The Prophet Nahoom
With Concubine

After a hoist winter
move ahead into town
carrying the long view
wind in the cows' bellies
anyway the dope crop
with too much colour
for sizeable knuckle
insert black yellow brown
run out of seed
in the same field
use another kind

What other news
except the music
tents visible
along the river
nocturne with falling
zeppelin

7
Marley Speaks

hanging to the side of this one
and almost measurable
in other words placing scarce lives
at the edge of giant buildings
even crocuses even natural
disasters even target calculations
tight within my proven injuries
dry dry facewind taking the first
flesh of moisture with it thick pollen
building up inside the bone mincer
music scraping the top language
layer from old circuits into grit
were I to heave my lines through
manchurian caravan routes
narrow mountain passes and keen
alleyways of Akbar they would still
find myopic traces with hot
dumb hatchings the green blue ordinance
of forbidden cities
                                        Ah Diana
(author author!) fame reigns
within the bituminous eaves
and wing walls also of your bed

8
Café Politik

down here warmth has eluded him as certain as
light coming through tree maze and other sliding
blue pen for proximity to sky black for earth
all arranged with dust and shavings over
wall to wall dream below pimple surface hangings
sure of nothing except soft flake snow
on ceilings thumb prints on full cigarette
packs tomorrow dustbins scheduled
for collection he hopes to see morning sun
penetrating dense words with some show
of concentration hard wedge of polish
over night time spirit slump
and total loss sad howl sad sacred city

through simplicity mouth of lion pen scrapper
crush! what chance have we left ourselves
to return from materia prima of language
good sticky architecture with warm cavities
for living in a chance to invent spring
running to cuddly dogs with soft elastic
exteriors high domed heads leading to limp
mouth and trimmed edge to the table's hearth rug
whereas out in the graveyard breaking
open the icy oblong definitions
this wolf landscape hacking away slowly
at reference and the dire burial of cannibal
confusion after correction

9
Fire Exits

this morning it comes back to me a giant palm
with braille oratory out of rubble versions
Lorca dragged through flowers in Andalucia
and a blazing illumination they are his songs
that brought him there also words with a shape
like guru which halted me in my progress
towards happy valerian the green overrun by pink
at last a new start breakfast is over
such grace such visits upon my ganglion tape
Bela walks with me will always be accompanied
and openness leads to my mind on triangular
dark cuts the chair engraves on blank snow
that is one marking method getting out another
over 3000 miles the windy Urals also influence
glucose experiments in Havana and some days
abandoned to the rain O'Hara gives himself
to feelings of friendship towards orange and easy
turns like: the: weeping: mise en scene: thank you

10
Back to the Beginning

that's me stop string carrier the spongy start
of a percussion escape from the old country salver
holoblastic altogether labial and passive

you see this already has a form in smooth blue
velvet so far down the woodland excerpt
hand in hand bird beaters step out chugging

onto the mouldering floor with stipend tiger
prowling in native compound professionally concerned
with crosshatch details and haunch dont you see

everything is explained in its own language
what was made in german is left in german
alfresco murals surrounded by tiny television hum
which emerges from nature as a contractual ob

ligation stop stop stop I can tell from the way
my bedside telephone looks it's a pile-up
I am last in line I have fears about the cold
my scoot devoid of its celebrated click talent

this is the least of it reading back much has already
suffered from resonant excision dust collecting
and sharp stanza breaks like dazed mahatmas
dealing out smoke in the high appalachian crinkle

IV

Tabellae Linnaei

15 poems of Linnaeus
by way of self-portrait

1 Leçon de Choses

the name Linnaeus
it having been mentioned
in connection with not sense
but the sound of it punting
against spectral pollution
the word *prose* comes to mind)
band aid stuck to the sole
of his shoe and then
there's that business of using
his teeth
his worship
(thank you Epikouros

starting now I wish to be
specific about vast landscape
plains of Manchuria for example:
twelve million blades of panic grass
motels at prehistoric maneaters
slides of conifers acting as stone
on an adjectival graph
follows
yen income units consumed
at a stage of sonic waste
where it angers him to be told
'oh, well...'

landscape is now
mainly a dolby button
with dependence on a great gas
of palates
(he who chose exempli gratia
to smudge Ketchum Idaho
with his left hand
end of world
[frame]
blood machine
paralysed in an ace pumping position
weather this time of year hitting
an age of accurate weltschmerz

as heavy water quantum
O field of veins! open to receive
plot control driven like a cleat
into smooth arctic wimple,   )

2 Last Poem

Stop, yes.
Breath naming.
Repertoire break within compounds
of moribund art so often
as skill ascribed falsely
to nature's continuum
power not enough credited
as is neither enough speed
word pain: spondee: third of a second
with all those swatch colours
coming at you fast
'destroyer & preserver'

So everything does measure
everything: dactylic
(hit it again Babette)
second version lost poem
He restraineth not his anger forever
Because he delighteth in mercy
rubbing out on the way
gummed tape his potala
spectator tint /smoke/
Xochipilli returning home
of all places a region despised
because it contains no gold
airing his legs in Linnaeus.

3 Opium War

vajra crown

bzzzzz tv

red passage
followed by
appearance of

silver
butterfly
upon
turquoise

dog not
spectrum
so costly
that image

papaver somniferum
to prevent sleep
from overtaking
can there be such delight in't
thus 'being' to be
a certain act of
sacral congruence
where death /smiling teeth/
in half light/your own
odorous *language* language

4 The Linnaeus Letters

halfway through the apple
it has already turned brown
winter preserving
                                        the woods also
the broken pencil

'swart sallow body'
these are your breasts

when you went
there were tea leaves
lurking *behind* the cup
la vie secrète
la mort imbécile

5 555

I begin to describe
slowly / slowly
smoke clears
the black harp
of my cigarette

harp! I barely
recognise spring
when it comes
binomials
green / green

instead Linnaeus
I burn holes
in your poem
while you write
mine

6 Doctrines

1. Carolus Linnaeus dying of tight fat
within genera tables heavy wine & dishes
chairs an agenda of water lilies this space
of binomial thresholds news of war
in a neighbouring sovereignty the sky black
every public book in his house open at p. 21
(not always in blue stump but sacrificial)
The wheatfields
of my distress
Clogged ponds
of inertia through which he sweats out
the probity of language as condemned property

what has *that* to do with *this*?
tired dispenser
pealing its old bell & my armpits worse today
than ever

Few people can say with any certainty
the dead measure
Linné the double axe
who heard voices such
and people running
at night and argued against breath
using it hard
like a crazy poet from Stockholm

2. How can we choose without him
making pineal constructs
out of pollen and indescribable stone
here among shelves leaves pages
the sun sparsely scuttled by script
from a run-out pen
also his crabbed left hand
O music my song
we are grown within an obliquity
beside scattered island waste
where each of us takes notes
from paraphic Canaanite signatures

forcing too many lines of beauty
so easily
            thy looks are passed away
like autumn
                and fills thy hand
                with dead vine

7 Moving Obbligato

speaking to her (rather, me)
since we allows for notation
delete and caret (I doubt
if that's what's intended here
shift has occured already
obbligato yes that's where
it belongs within which
my stinking exhortive muse
sitting here waiting for me
to click on the vegetation:
One...   spider plant
Two...   yarrow (pink)
Three... soul lennei
Four...   gross mystery
               but thick fleshy green
               with trunk supporting
               disproportionate leaves
               in relation to growth
and there you have it:
Linnaeus!

8 Desidua

I have taken it enough from books
why else do I find myself now
or just before each persuasion
waiting on poems in which references
have appeared soundfully as leaves
without the sense of it within the word
Linnaeus

(You would understand this sacrifice)

Throwing cheap gold on to railway lines
flattening myself against speed
& shamanic doctrines like God
beginning with beth always wordy
who has prepared this stroke
for slaughter
                          a bicycle alone revolves
in the pit throwing out flushes
of mechanical insight into vegetal
confusion
                      One hears them: chain brake
crossbar spoke rubber pedal bell
oh summer! you throw yourself across
my throat my hair singing with white wasps
ascending from the deciduous oil of his hearth

9 Borders of Rococo

Infancy, you must be dead by now
having left anyway by about 1925
hard, monodic
                                        and my hand too
whereof was gold upon
the pages of talmudic Babylon
'supremist example of weight & shape'
death the guise how these words
abominate me even as there is
no other black within which
I can stop pursuing you

Linnaeus, physician
                                        who does permit us
access to your surgery
                                        I exhort my eyes, my lips
in rage: the act of your fallibility
your doctrinal sacrifice
                                        stooping thus
to your patients
who desire nothing nothing
but to love your dominion

10 For the Last Time

Stop killing the tuberoses
I don't mind about the children
going
        they are so gorgeous anyway
I see their faces pasted up
against memorial stones
as dead as buttonholes

Pain words surround us thus night
but will not stop the flare of those flowers
from lighting the seams of Perth Amboy
Esther's farm which held them
white white I remember easier than shape
in charitable hard-worked slime
so good that brindle falls
having such an appearance of reality
across the idea of summer
and summer itself
                    which catches lines
coming of vapour and usage and presses them
against my ragged door
The Book of Linnaeus

11 Water

He was no artist
a user of sylvan often
in rose madder
increasingly
hard to locate
either in nature
or fact

I do not love you
'painted from life'
you are a word
lodges in my
aqueous throat
'...looking for a house
along water'
Linnaeus
when you pass you
look in at the rain
falling across this blue door

Blue: a further excision
(he reads what he has drawn)
cuts language down to breath
esparto grass drawing blood after it
across his tongue questions
as to who commands
this eloquent compound

12 First Pull

Paged oblique against English light
oily black letterpress and I know
enough to read perhaps 2 words:
acknowledge, subjective. How can
anyone use *pantheism?* Also somewhere
in the middle of sorts relating to
cranes fleeing south for warmer
'climes', yes, a semi-colon and blue
sky laying in a harvest of wheat,
stooks and all this Linnaean
paraphernalia I have my hands full of.
Oh shape me before it is too late
and I learn to live with your colours.

13 Linné on Öland

How each of your sheets
you covered to the edge
with pollen!
                    sommar
as I have seen it on this island
where displaced stones in cairns
30 metres long, 3 metres high
still not clearing the fields
for more than scrub juniper
and a table deep enough for one poem
at a time

                In consequence of Linnaeus
the naming of parched orchis, scarab
and wild valerian
                        if I am right
about even that

As I begin she brings
a vase for my poem
as though I know them:
yarrow, larkspur, some red poppy
which sings in the heat of the room,
yellow buttons
                    and cornflower

One of the sounds here is the Baltic Sea
and I must not smile so much at that
for in the crevasses and wood
as of death, the wind, the wind
like the lines which live
in my desolate mouth
opening lips against your yet disparate
tabulations
                (anent those yellow buttons:
renfana or *chrysanthemum vulgare*
describing with a scent
of sweet paraffin

how much there is of your need
as giving me such runic
approximations to joy within
the spiky circle of my pen

14 The Island

As they cannot make openings easily
in the rock soil, the women scatter
pine needles over their own faeces
and of their families...'

Linnaeus, 1741

This bitch of an island
dry sliver to my tongue
slips into top gear
another language engaged
and it comprises the whole
of Linnaeus:
stone, calx,
the vociferous berries
and broad arses breaking over
shit heaps on soil 15 cm deep
under blue flowers, green trumpets,
the golden storms, all sky
plummeting down onto rock
and lichen with such clamp
as coming home is
And the children:
their blinding whiteness

15 Opus Posthumous

I am finished with Linnaeus:
it has been like placing coins, matches,
paper under one leg of an uneven table
unsure, though it doesn't matter,
if it's the floor or the table leg
which has its certain inept bias.

In the best sense, I mean corpus,
I'm no longer dealing happily in matters
of spirit or psyche or even logic.
Too much has been said already
about those stations;
there's a place for that.

It's time to read it again.
I have no way to understand
what my mind is telling me to do.
I do it, it falls around me like
this rain which has covered everything all week
dead centre between Rochdale and Burnley.

Let me put it this way:
the sky suddenly goes black, thunderous,
the telephone rings and as I walk
across the room to answer it
(I know it can be nothing but marvellous
disaster) it stops and I stand there

in the centre of the room's grip waiting
for it to ring again and it doesn't.
Where does that leave *you*?
another question: why did it ring?
It's not as though I have been away
that long or plan to go again, far.

V

North Light

– I saw nobody coming, so I went instead.
– John Berryman, from 'Henry's Confession'

He Does What He Can

Thus he puts out the light the garbage
this always leads to language
(the words have a similarity
of rhythm, a certain
mouth structure, a certain
realtionship to God, for instance)
then, alone, he takes out his teeth
kisses them and practises
a kind of flawed fiction
sibilance fills his room
he believes the house next to his
is being used for the convenience
of machinery
                    So be it
since we have begun all of us
to accept the fact of spatial worlds
a cracking up
                    a certain dryness

Depending on its colour
he uses the word *stanza* or *stencil*
to describe every thing he sees:
overlooking his tiny garden
at the back (this novel of venal supremacy)
5 white stanzas of a children's ward
with pink stencils at every window
                                        (O come, look)
Monday morning les dames aux peignoirs
such a tiny sea across which
he sails with stubby pads
at the helm writing poems
and reminiscences in subjunctive
grammar
                Is this, commands old dentures,
the only way to drown?

Gateway

soft rage that music hangs up spit
among cold bougainvillea in hot
monody oft the words solo voce
o death it has been on my shoulder
where you are tropical dame
animal disc slogan
there's no fun in't cunt
though I love you more (struck
(replac'd/*and* I love it more
each day passeth deeper into
this crumbling brick house
that surrenders me evenly
transferring from one hand
that giveth and yours which
has already passed to within
mine own quiet fist

Silesia

mythically it resists etch
Goths rise from the sea
and I have already
densed its plumb line
with the language
of linen somehow
it is green in my mind
everywhere castellations
have applied description
bright glistening along black
and here is where my heart
becomes involved with smoke
and turncoat and lays down
with the werewolf poem
its scissors its gateway
its bloody progress

Carriage Return

after a short journey
the door gets sacrificed
to brevity you naiads
I would imitate your voice
rasp adze azimuth
everything that has to do
with kitchen craft
seizing me as an unattainable
gift

in this corner now I exaggerate
the sparrows my glass heavier
than when I started although
I have been drinking (whisky)
for the past 30 years some
times
        a
   lone

'Between Us'

When I say that spacing counts for everything
I do not refer necessarily to that narrow plane
between your eyes or the distance
which exists between your coming in
and later your coming in again as though
you were someone I knew once
                                                            my life is yours
you balance it like a geomancer telling me
some things give themselves to measure at least
that I have done so and so resulting
inevitably in a congruence which I have tried
to avoid all my life and I do not like
being told that this long enactment we share
is heroism or a page of holy indolence
though I can see it is somewhere
in the syntax of pride
                                        or love

Spin Off Spinoza

can't you see that I have a share
in your purchase of lucidity
when you come with me into pastures
of cornflower & red poppy
& think that as you emerge
from darkness you will those
flowers into inference then flesh

on the other hand you cannot bring
music to this language you use
& despite the sun which moves
over your house travelling
from one obliqueness of ground
to its opposite refraction
'...who knows the passion of Bach
but does not its reason...'
you capture the quick-sleeved
apparency of light the pleasure
of its corrosive celibacy

Bokhara

to Owen Davis

The differences between us Owen
or one of them, the least,
is that I did not know
the dead mouse you lamented
in your long compassionate poem

My room is windy
my poems brief
whereas I believe –
though I cannot be sure,
I surmise it from your constant smile –
your house contains
a wife two children
a certain type of human
double protection glass

But I may be wrong
about that, it is possible
my poems are windy too
that they suffer the same seizure
you may be enduring
in a house full of broken windows

but your songs
your songs
by way of hieroglyph

Now I do mean the reciprocation
of your language, its questing deployment,
the way it developes
in
  mid
air
and seizes me
with the same
                    clarity
de dum de dum it goes along

I see myself always working soft signs
in a hard climate, this for example,
trees dead, spondaic rock
and how these words abominate us
so what I lose
is narrative
& brevity
& (just for the look of it)
colour

I find lately in order to do
first I remove my teeth
the bandages from my window
across the valley a hard fist
breaks light and makes known
malodorous fictions
de dum de dum it goes as such
                                        chorister rhetoric
glaucoma retching at the sight
of colour making its crippled way
down to the Calder bow
which looks concrete enough in water
I look up the same Latin references
not understanding structure
how girls who edge on promontories

are more in my mind than ever
profiles lighting cigarettes
in a fierce wind looking towards
Denmark
                drawing me to them,
as Odysseus knew, with their songs
de dum
            their
                    songs

Infield Outfield

Who sees the curve as Robert Fludd saw it
or Zukofsky
                    going back further
as did Hank Greenberg the Bronx hitter
moved like deer round the ballgame
smudging all the bases
                                        (speaking
of childhood at this point
                                              on loan:
memorabile) like music
which curves along the galleries
                                                        as though
we *come* to it so
                              that is, the mind curved
...not mind itself but as in Duccio, say,
flat against flat green
as it *was* then, as he saw it,
not so much as concept however
but as matter...
aagh, that impenetrable slag and iron
and light as it cuts its way through
– the poem without shape –

or money, say, or the stupidity
of government, the long aimlessness
as that forest for the first time
approaching Hardcastle Crags
climbing high & time believing
it will lead to silky rain not as reward
but justice as within the avoidance of it
on macadam
                    just another road
and around here that means
Keighley
                or some other benevolence
like a blow to the tongue

Chipping out the Heat

In this centre camp the ink is blackest.
I stamp everything with it: ALGERIA:
clogs, camel leather, kangaroo bags, individual
mummies, passages from the ziggurats
of Eastern Africa and ceremonial staffs.
It goes for humans too: HEREWITH:
their songs, their deletions, their embraces,
their intentions in the areas of art, henna
& the signs they place at stoups & fountains,
their alluvial aspirations before the shunting
fire gods who in passing smear the scorch
of worship, contemptuous of gold & invocation.

But humping his innocence the headman
prints out my lodgings within the enclave
of buffalo maidens.
                                        They are inviolable,
sensitive to my forms of literature,
possessed by a somewhat dispassionate calligraphy.
I'm not concerned about all this arduous
admiration.
                        What I have described so far
is the simplicity of paradise.
                                                            It opens its arms,
it is fictive; precise; and sleeps in the punctuation
of desirable sunlight.

Now I know what city we are in.
                                                    There are signs of it
in the way a book opens always to the right passage
which goes down accurately between one line
& that gate which holds fullsome meadow
in its own place.
                                I mean, as you have already
passed me in a pursuit of not wisdom
but certainty, I hand you this cluttered
vocabulary of kisses
                                    though you have it all

already in the sleight of your hands,
your throat like a garb of punctures
woven by my loose splintered idiom.

Il Pleut

Oh I can do it figuratively too.
Sometimes I can write it no other
way!
          the fingerboard black & white
for me, for you perhaps;
                                        I can't say.
Euclid, dominie, I see him
blind along the battlements of
clear thinking.

                        It rains,
TV has been turned on
in the other room;
                              it's the child.
I get up, cap the pen, join him
where the screen is always purple.
Verlaine speaks to him,
                                    not to me.
'What do you think?' I ask
as he flies towards Hebden flow,
out the window in the direction
of Stoodley Pike
                              playing Art Tatum
solos to the most convincing
descriptions
                  of death.

'DENSE, DENSE.'

She Passes Through the Poem

Aggie

I did not own
even the gesture my hand was
made of, or the measure
of her shoulder through
the elegance of itself,
the bowed bone,
the possession
of edict, the semiotic
placing of uncial
to its rightful line;
of letters and their shadows
and all the beauty
of passage.

I am beginning
to resemble those who have insisted
they do not stand in the field
my poems occupy.
I do not know
this poem yet, for example,
or its rabid structure.
But at least I am not alone
in the abuses of thews
and flowers and music
which are there of their own
winding and all the paraphernalia
of speech and so on.

In light and darkness
and her sweet presences
which travel to us:
out of the forest
the boundaries
the doors.

Acknowledgements

I would like to thank the editors of the following magazines, books and anthologies in which many of these poems were first published: *Ambit, Analect, Antioch, Ants Forefoot, A Part Apart* (The White Dog Press), *Big Jewish Book* (Doubleday), *Branch Redd, Breakfast, Cavanagh's Press, Edge* (Joe DiMaggio), *e.g. series* (Norwich School of Art), *European Judaism, Figs, Ink, Loaded Drum, Loose Use* (Pig Press), *Miscellaneous, New Departures, Saintly Fingers, Second Aeon, Shelter, Sixpack, Southwest Review, Spot Press Cards, Steam Press, Terraplane, Time Being* (Blue Chair), *Transatlantic Review, Tree, Wallrich cards.*

A B